From Paris,
Lost Vegas,
Home again

From Paris,
Lost Vegas,
Home again

Arthur Jackson V

WESTBRAE LITERARY GROUP

ISBN: 979-8-9917199-2-6
Published by Westbrae Literary Group
Berkeley, California
Jon-David Hague, Founding Editor

For more information about this and other titles from
Westbrae Literary Group, visit us at westbraeliterarygroup.com or
email us at info@westbraeliterarygroup.com

In dedication to my brother in arms, and fellow poet – Ido. It is his advice and/challenge of my work that keeps me on my toes. My best friend Veronica for always listening to me read poetry, and reminding me I'm not crazy, I'm an artist. My Mom & Pops for their unrelenting support. And last but not least, my friend Nathan. Without him my first trip to Paris (where this collection begins) may have never happened. Thank you for always believing in me.

CONTENTS

From Paris

Lost Vegas

Frisco-Kid

From Paris

To Refuse Divine Donation

Yesterday I found myself believing in God, sitting in Notre Dame praying après donating 2€ for a tea light candle; lighting it with a long already used stick charred with the prayers of tourists before before. After praying I even Catholic kiss-crossed my chest&head. In a culture I wasn't yet apart of I felt involved, all encompassing so ritual.

There were larger candles to take after you donated, but, I didn't want to give 2 more euros despite the stand clearly reading in 4 languages "Donating is completely up to you" «C'est votre choisie se donner deux €». It felt like the mirror in an unaccompanied candy bowl at Halloween; tricking kids to only take one treat (take only what is needed). Maybe I rather not disrespect whatever it was that inspired all those architects&artists and praying voices who made up Notre Dame. Alhamdulillah.

Arrondissement 16

You wouldn't know it unless you were one of us with an affinity for walking, but, cruising- that which has been reduced to a myth in San Francisco in recent generations does still exist beyond an app in Paris. I went - listening to Prince; dancing through the foliage of a forest of a park, a little treasure of quiet green. He caught me there, stuck staring into a petrified tree twined and draped in spiderwebs thick enough to be threads on their own. He stopped and watched me wonder

/is this how spiders do it, catch their prey with the tricks of dangerous beauty?/

He too was caught, tricks are sometimes shared stones between birds. I turned a droit and he cocks his head back; a greeting and proposition.

We both become webbed with each other. Il me dit

«*/Je gentil avec toi, pas de probleme/*» with a soft voice and my hand on his cock. He walked forwards walking me backwards */face a face/* into the shadows of trees where condom wrappers littered the ivy like sequin - */can a bit of earth be so queer?/* The way the light fractures their colors on our skin, it must have the ability.

Il deja dit «/*gentile avec toi*/» kissing the syllables to my forehead and neck just behind the ear. I remembered Erykah Badu singing about wanting for a man to whisper there.

Grenade

In France they call a pomegranate
 un grenade
Crack, burst & splash red

I've been living here a little over a month now
and have since forgotten the perpendicular view of arriving
Maybe, it is time to go
I'm tired of unfolding cafe tables
I don't tire quickly

Crack; the henge
Splash; the rain
Dust buzz everywhere

Wasps all over my hands for sugar

Has this left a bad taste?
                no, none of it
But, I'll still proceed with caution
there's a cactus on the wall
that sharpens for its pricks

Better for the splash
defensive tricks
ripe grenade

I think it's time to go
there may be landmines

BURST

I was in Paris
Bladder about burst
hosing down a wall
to relieve the pressure under
my abdomen   The bar
bouncer caught me &
wouldn't let me in

I had only wanted cheap beer
& trivia in a language I
half understood

And somehow
I was still head-over-heels   And
somehow I am still head-over-heels   And some
How
I found his pride romantic

«love me enough to not disrespect me
What burning we could cultivate»

Sometimes I wish I'd just let myself
BURST

But that would be the least French
thing I could do

I hope upon returning to the bar
he says «I remember you»

Out of Sight Out of Mind

Where do we birth guilt?
Where do we push it out?
I refuse to tell him
I'm leaving Paris early
In my head
after Septembre
he'll show up
with his hasheesh
to the bookstore
only to share
with some other
green haired boy

Hopelessly, Tragically, Romantic

I've been working
on quieting the roses

When I pick
them they scream
On a frequency

I've been trying
to find posies
but turn up
ashes beneath the rosebeds

to replace dirt

I found your ring
You lost it
I found it

Under my pillow
after you left Paris
for London

After saying goodbye
with two kisses

your ring swings
on my ear

Lately I've been searching
the pockets for their posies
to exchange for a parler

avec toi
tu me manques
Do you remember our words
opening us

like a chrysalis

The morning I returned
from Venice
Amilia and I ran
down rue de la Bouchérie
screaming your name

Found you slugging two
suitcases in thrifted shoes
a few steps from the metro

The Kisses We Touch Our Lips to Remember

                                        Isn't that sweet?
A lipfull embrace of a moment

Time become horcrux
Horcrux becomes a piece of you
You graze your lips
to recall that piece of yourself

We carry timestamps
on our skin
Don't you remember the last grimace?
the early laugh

Joy bloomed to sky
and outcries to showless gods

Even your hands clasped

                                        in prayer

leaves a wear on your fingerprints
It is said your ancestors trauma
is logged in your DNA

There is a medical trace

                                        to a memory

Venice

It was hotter than hell
even though we
were on an island surrounded
by little islands
by water

We arrived to Venice by
way of raspberry vines
that became driftwood
following our train to dock

The city with outdoor restaurants
draped in grapevines

It was sinking unnoticeably
I drowned myself in gelato
He reminded me how sorrow
can hug you
from behind like a friend
disguised by a wonder

And when we got lost
in the venetian maze
I would run my fingers
along the walls

They crumbled to ruin
then dust
becoming history catching wind

Lost Vegas

Resurface

Sometimes I feel like I'm
       drowning
in a reality that belongs to someone
       else
my mother   maybe,
some artist who lost
his-their
way
           maybe . . .

For eight years I concurred water
          maybe more. I dive
head first,
I swim
     "But you have job security" they say
     But I need soul security I feel

A flame is buried deep within me. I need
a reason, un devoir

      Some Phoenix flame; awaken my flappy wings
        Flapper boy in green

        I need to break the water . . .
         Surface

Sea-Legs

How do we forget our brightness?

Is it this?

Light pours from our eyes
instead of down on to us. So,
when this light we give
off shines on others- in
our sight - it becomes
theirs
Should we stop staring so much?
Take to the sea
maybe, gain sealegs
Take to a renaissance
learn of water births
how to become light-full

waking out of the sea coming to shore
shining.

The Still Life of Lush

I am halfway into a Manhattan
stogue pinned
between spider leg fingers
a sidecar on the way
Work of the day
done, and worthless

The job is supposed to help
in this land of dreams

But it's landed me at the bar
a lush for an escape
a bucket of fries and
Why is nothing ever smooth

sidecar crashes down my throat
ice chills my teeth

                              I want to quit

but an exit doesn't pay the bills
tolerance does
Tolerance renders me an expensive date
and a worker with a problem

Textures

Glass likes shatter

                                      simple

Apple likes bite

                                      crisp

My phone likes your number

                             Taps become
                         Clicks become
                           Lips become
                           Hips become
                               Sips

from your pelvis

My hands become a bowl
I scoop from your body
I learn the meaning of taste

                               How permeate you

me   Do storm clouds soak up the ocean

before rain?

                         heavy with a shadow

Glass

Old windows were made of molten
glass spun into a flatness
This left them with
a slight bow that
grows as it
ages and
becomes
a shade
of g-
old

Soot or Snow

I cannot help but punctuate each breath
with «why?»
Every day is so full of question
                    «what am I doing here?»
                        «where am I going?»
                    «what do I want, anymore?»

            «why was this cloud birthed my vertical?»

What do I do with morning?
I'm too empty for breakfast;
                an empty stomach coffee makes sick.
and, God I WANT SOME GOOD DICK
                    and god I want some good dick
The sun smells of genesis
                                or ash
at least it comes as snow

Morning Prayers

Was I undressed by morning?

                           Apollo's warm hands

was coffee the first thing

                  ready, black

                 The thick smell fills
                    the room

The sound of yawns

                   melic rise

There was light coming
through blinds

                  Petit warm lies
                through shaded lines

             they glow on this brown skin

          Is this how we show up to prayer?
I remember being in Paris&burning

               candles for prayer

Light came différent
Bathing the ovine in color

             Tinted through aged glass
            bloated by the clout of men
              in white robes

swinging sage smoke
to fill the halidom

An Italian woman spilled
herself before the holy corp
Strung up on a cross
I asked myself
«how much faith does that take?»

Never felt that
Never craved that
Never prayed that way
Never prayed that
Never prayed
Never

Des Pommes

I remember Notre Dame waking me at 6h00 tous des matins
                              Bells become bon jour
                        The perfume of coffee comes in currents
                        when I crack open the double windows
                            sunlight showers my brown skin
It glows
                                My chest hairs yawn
I remember confirming the lollipop trees existing
                        I remember the taste of my first croissant
                            sopping up the gold rise of morning
                    even the silver colony of the migrating clouds
& the cigarette smoke of the homeless man
                dragging his blackened feet down rue de la bucherie

I remember the silence of 8h30
punctuated by the scuffling claws of rats
                            Did you ever watch Tom and Jerry
as a child?
                        I called the rats Jerry's because they
                            held the same audacity

                    Nothing stayed silver long at this hour
                        before movement gained momentum

Before cameras send parades of flashes over brides

outside this old bookshop

when Notre Dame is across the street

Where did love become an Instagram
filter?

How did we forget to smile from our kidneys

into the eyes of our apples?

We picked them for their sweetness

We picked them for nourishment

They stayed until they were gone

Either eaten or rot

then seed the earth and now we have a tree

for any to pick and be fed

like we

No one starves!

And we've all participated in an orchard

The Day Dorothy Missed Oz

I am drinking Hennessy

                                        Black&

eating Lays

                        Waves tinged orange with fake cheese

wondering

                « What the fuck? »

I miss San Francisco

I miss the piss smelling streets

                         The golden showers

I miss my girls

                    Their kisses that warmed me
                      like the first puff of weed
                        when we rolled green

I miss the green

                      We puffed so much atop

Dolores, the scene   panoramic

                      San Francisco, my Bitch
                      Henny hitting

I am far from home petting my dog

                      naming him Baby Boy

Remembering Daddy's calling me Boy

before I sip them, yeah I miss that,

too

I miss watching the Castro sign lit up drunk
Sometimes the 'O' or 'R' would be MIA

                        I don't remember which
Bulb dun forgotten current
to light the way for this Faggot

                        Even that pulls at the space
                    where my heart waits for Muni
Take me somewhere
Right now, the radio sings

                 « Could it be I'm falling in love »
This Henny is loving
to remind me home

                    too expensive
                 too changed in the last
                   five years, well

Frisco-kid

Were the World Mine

I haven't written in a long time
and that's really sad
but were the world mine
there would be trees as tall
as the eye can see and
they would grow syllables
the taste of Christmas morning
my friends would
gather them on their
harvesting tongues
and they would taste like lavender honey they
my friends would share them to grow
forests where we kiss each other
with swollen lips and paint each other
with wealthy hands my friends
painting each other
the colors of a hungry sky
being fed by morning
my night
would be filled with a thumping and bass
and what a gracious night
and disco lights
the ground
the dance floor vibrate
From all the stomping her feet in

and shaking those thighs creating a sweat
dripping down their backs
what rain
what storm
were the world mine
our dance would create storms
Were the world mine
our love would create a storm
whose rain tastes like the first step
on the dance floor
when you hear your favorite song
I want stanzas that sound like
swallowing a lovers tongue
in the middle of a crowded dance floor
Haven't you ever done that?
Glitter smeared across
your chest
gin & tonic
running down your arm
Confused if the sway of you is drunk
or in rhythm
I wanna go back outside
for not work reasons
and smell a fucking parade
Were the world mine again
my friends
we'd run a fucking parade through Mother Earth

and we'd call her our bitch
because she's our friend too!
And she'd tell us all about her tattoos

«Some city slick kid made some graffiti on a sidewalk
of laughter because he missed the vibing of a gather»

Who wants to gather with me?!
Were the world mine
I'd have a truck big enough
for all our dreams
and I'd pick up all my friends
and we'd paper-mâché
what love tasted like the first time it came by
and make a float
for Fucking parade
Look out Market st.
some cool Kats
are comin' your way!"

This Just in:

We first met Under fuchsia light
we spun poetry weblike
all Ginsberg and Tatum
Queerness was the "Happening"

Bathed all that pink
but, fuchsia eventually fades

I did everything
to be a friend

The things that friends do

While he
tracing a box
around me
A box that was really a house
The house had walls
Those walls dressed in wallpaper

The wallpaper of pretty things

Outside
he was weaving spider webs
What trickery

and trapped
Just in.
Bathed in pink
the view looks like spilling tea

Now, I'm just a little black widow
in a little black house, Justin
Now, I'm just a little black widow
in a little black house Just
in: I'm a Little Black Widow
in a Little Black House
whose pincers seep pink venom
due to light exposure

Tequila & Blood Orange

yesterday, tulips grew from my pupils
the irises, soil

                                        watered

a violent spring

too much rain

eyes bloodshot
         face swollen
                  room   cold

you could feel the temperature drop
even the heater rattled like gravel
turned it off - the sound
worse than the cold, and
it wasn't working anyway

there was a whiff of tequila & sparkling blood orange
and the sound of vacancy was deafening

Grow Where You are Planted

[for Miki]

Imagine if I didn't count
my shame before sleep
Imagine how light
my shoulders would be
Imagine if I could
actually sleep

If I knew peace
for a pillow

It's become a ritual

I lay down
        my mind retraces
                my steps
                        I cringe

One day –the moment before
I die
I will regret a lifetime
Every shame will be a particle
that makes up my grave-
stone «Here lies Arthur Jackson
V of his name
under all this dirt»

Every grain - a shame
every foot between six - a history
of nights looking
at the ceiling. Gravedigger shovels
them to fill a hole
I'm finally asleep
Finally shameless

When I die I
want to be planted
as a tree
so I can continue
to grow
even after I'm gone

Dante & Virgil

You taste like grapefruit lingers
in vodka
You bite like the back end
This is the first night we spun like sugar
around our spines
This is the first night we
spun like sugar
This is the first night
you spun your tongue round
mine and I creased
like a candy wrapper
'round hard candy
Lust has an aggressive lick
I wanted to kiss you while throwing darts
in back a bar

You taste like Felix Felicis

and again I fold

Lattice Weave

grasp my neck while we walk
grab the back of my waist band
ride your bike along side my stride
call me bonic   call me baby
i headbutt you

        you headbutt me
     mess up my hair, then
       kiss me
          kill me
fuck softly   then we
       fuck hard

did you know gold is a metallic lattice?
     you glow like honey

      weave with me

You always spelling sew incorrectly

i wanna make out with everyone
i would kiss the moon
had it lips
i would kiss the fucking moon
all we do is orbit at parties
dancing circles in dark skies
surrounded by stars
this poem is about no one
about everyone
don't feel special
we are all made of stardust
some of us are just better at glowing
and sharing luminescence
when i kiss the moon i'm kissing you
let's run like 6 year olds on candy canes
love me lavishly
love me lavishly
you beautiful satellite, you
stop trying to see faces in the moon
this poem is about no one
and everyone
i'm gonna kiss the moon one day
i'm gonna be a star
as above
Sew below

Spit

[memory mixtape]

I am on my knees
looking up at him reclining
hands clasped behind his head
                    wondering how he smiles that way
;menacing and gentle

                    «Boy . . . » he says

                    A build of sweat collects
                    in a small patch of hair
                    above my crack

The petrichor of the room
is sweeter than usual
I admire his armpits
                    My lips part
                    I let out a small
breath

He spits at my face
                    it rains a fine mist

The corners of my mouth
retrace the steps of a smile

He releases his fingers
using one hand to touch my face
                    his hands are rough

                Sweat drips from that
              small patch down my crack
                  to land on a star
                this creates a shiver

He places his thumb
I'm my mouth

            «Open, that tongue is mine now»

I offer him his tongue
He spits again

Clumsy Me

I bump into things   like
    all the time
Corners   The night
    stands edge   my
    head
      against

        a wall

Clumsy little black boy
Never grasp the sand boy
Never wants the party to end boy

always holds his breath
before pressing send
        Hold your breath
        Count to three

Letters always leave weird sugar on your tongue

The way they taste like the edge
        of

           leaving

You found me at the edge and called
my name like succeeding Mount Everest
We, nephilim

Red giants
only took two years to become nova

«I heard it takes two years come down from that
beautiful place; I heard it's so nice»

Was so bright and
all glow and heat
I knew needle and thread but   You
showed me so
                    Lucky me

blow out the candles

for John B.

I feel like my brain has been   put
on pause on stand by   I'm
waiting for shit to make sense.
I feel both
    piled
on and swept
under the rug

             "Nothing ever lasts forever"

Remove the _ever_ and it makes more sense
         Nothing is the longest relationship

The final girl
      wooden stakes
         esteem & strength
           and witty catchphrases

I thought that was me   I
was my stories Pink Opaque Buffy
Maybe I still am and THIS is the illusion
Am I being beaten by illusion?

Is life just illusion?
Am I in a chaotic
              DMT
              coma locked
              slumber sleep
                                        Am I asleep?
Life is but an dream and
he don't want me
                      no more   Hard back!
My friend just O.D.'d

        And I wanna wake up from this
        dream   I can't catch my breath
        He took off the mask
        our kiss is gone gone gone. John
                    Insecure lion pockets full of
                    alphabet curves & acrylic paint

        Tell me! Why does love always stain
                when it's poured all over you?

I wish I could scrub the stretch
of death off of me   All
the grains John B. buried
underneath. Forever eulogized
in his Van Gough brush strokes
white knuckling the brushes
Impasto to be loved; Opalescent light house

Call all four corners
of the storm *on me*
Down on me
Lie open wide. Four empty corners
where four elements should be

Why is stardust just swept
under the rug?

Premature blow of a candle
O u   t
Should still be burning

Twist the Bones and Bend the Back

Everything is melting with me-   Lately

I

lately I've been sugar   I lately

I've

Been licked- syrupie spit   lately

I

lately I have dripped down your chin
Sticky & sweet

Lately

I have been sticky and sweet   -Me! I?
Recently? No, Lately I have been lost
No map no compass insignificant
wading through darkness
This incessant spinning

I

Lately I've spun; been whirling and
wrung and twisted

and twisted
and twisted-   SEE! I lately
I can't stop lately I am stuck
Lately I have been playing vampire
Lately I can't see myself
"Who's that guy?"   I lately
have been biting my own neck
recycling syrup

(63)

Lately I have been stuck
I want to suck out the marrow
of life so my bones stop breaking with a twist
>I'm tired of twisting
>Overworked and spent
>I have been weak
I have been broken
I have been burdened
>"Who is that guy?"
>That's not like me

You'll find me where the ink dries

I'm doing this pen and paper thing again
so I may recognize my own reflection

These familiar flicks leave familiar stains

How else do we remind ourselves our name?
How else do we remind ourselves our own name?

I script myself by Arthur
Stronger than a reflection

I trust my hand I don't trust my eyes
I'm always doing double takes,

in the mirror-
you're only supposed to believe half of what you see
So maybe I'll have seen myself once by looking twice
So maybe I'll have seen myself once

Fin.